Kitchen Science

Peter Pentland and
Pennie Stoyles

CHELSEA HOUSE
PUBLISHERS

A Haights Cross Communications | Company

Philadelphia

This edition first published in 2003 in the United States of America by Chelsea House Publishers, a subsidiary of Haights Cross Communications.

Chelsea House Publishers
1974 Sproul Road, Suite 400
Broomall, PA 19008-0914

The Chelsea House world wide web address is www.chelseahouse.com

Library of Congress Cataloging-in-Publication Data

Pentland, Peter.
    Kitchen science / by Peter Pentland and Pennie Stoyles.
    p. cm. — (Science and scientists)

Includes index.
Summary: Surveys some of the scientific principles related to foods and their preparation.

ISBN 0-7910-7014-X
1. Cookery—Juvenile literature. [1. Science—Miscellanea. 2. Cookery—Miscellanea.]
I. Stoyles, Pennie. II. Title.
TX652.5 .P395 2003
641.5'01'5—dc21

                                                    2002001280

First published in 2002 by
MACMILLAN EDUCATION AUSTRALIA PTY LTD
627 Chapel Street, South Yarra, Australia, 3141

Copyright © Peter Pentland and Pennie Stoyles 2002
Copyright in photographs © individual photographers as credited

Edited by Sally Woollett
Text design by Nina Sanadze
Cover design by Nina Sanadze
Illustrations by Pat Kermode, Purple Rabbit Productions

Printed in China

Acknowledgements
Cover: Chilies, courtesy of Steve Lovegrove.

Shafer & Hill/Peter Arnold/Auscape, pp. 5 (bottom right), 20–21; Science Pictures/Oxford Scientific Films/Auscape, p. 11 (top); Coo-ee Historical Picture Library, p. 18; Coo-ee Picture Library, pp. 14, 17 (right), 22–23, 23 (bottom), 27 (top); Joss Dimock, p. 13 (top); Getty Images/Photodisc, pp. 4–5, 6 (left), 15, 20 (left), 23 (top); Imageaddict, p. 26; Legend Images, pp. 25, 28–29; Steve Lovegrove, pp. 6–7, 8, 10, 11 (bottom), 13 (bottom), 16 (left), 27 (bottom), Museum of Victoria, p. 12; Terry Oakley/Picture Source, pp. 16–17; Dale Mann/Retrospect, p. 9; Southern Images/Silkstone, p. 24; Nick Osborne/Tasmanian Photo Library, p. 5 (top right).

While every care has been taken to trace and acknowledge copyright the publisher tenders their apologies for any accidental infringement where copyright has proved untraceable.

Contents

Glossary words

When a word is printed in bold you can look up its meaning in the Glossary on page 31.

Science terms

When a word appears like this **dissolved** you can find out more about it in the science term box located nearby.

Have you ever wondered...

...why a cake rises when it is baked?

...what causes food to go bad?

Did you know that all the answers have something to do with science?

...what makes up a balanced diet?

...how a microwave oven works?

Science in your kitchen

Kitchens are all about food. Many people prepare and cook food in their own kitchens. But they also buy food that is already prepared from a supermarket or restaurant. This food is prepared in large commercial kitchens.

Whether the kitchen is large or small, there is a lot of science going on in there. Food is made of chemicals, and **chemical reactions** occur when you mix ingredients together to bake a cake or make a curry. You also use chemicals to clean up the mess afterwards.

Often when you read in the newspaper or watch the news, chemicals seem to be something bad in our lives. This is only true of a very few chemicals.

Scientists

People have been experimenting for hundreds, even thousands, of years with different cooking ingredients and methods. They worked out better ways of making tasty and nutritious food without knowing the science behind what they were doing. Today, scientists and engineers have developed many of the tools and appliances used in the kitchen. Research into what foods are best for our health uncovers new information all the time.

There are many types of food scientists, and they all have different jobs to do.

- Dieticians study diets and **nutrition**.
- Chemists study chemicals and their reactions.
- Microbiologists study tiny **organisms** such as **bacteria**, viruses and **fungi**.

In this book you will:

- find out what happens when food is cooked
- meet a food scientist
- learn how appliances such as microwave ovens and refrigerators work
- understand why food goes bad and how to prevent this.

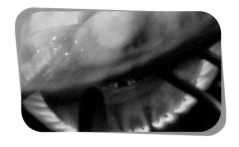

How does cooking work?

Have you ever eaten a raw potato or uncooked rice? Which is softer—raw or cooked carrot? What is the difference between toast and bread?

Foods are cooked for different reasons. You cook foods to:

- change their taste
- soften them so that they are easier to chew and digest
- remove some of the moisture to make them crisp
- change them from a liquid to a solid (or the other way around).

The energy to cook this food comes from charcoal.

Heat for cooking

Cooking always involves heat and it can be done in lots of ways. The heat usually comes from gas, electricity or charcoal.

Heat is a form of **energy**. One of the big rules in science is that you cannot create or destroy energy. You can just turn it from one type of energy into another. So how do you get heat?

Burning

Natural gas and charcoal are called fuels. Fuels contain stored energy. This is sometimes called chemical energy. When fuel burns, the chemical energy turns into heat energy. Burning requires a fuel and two other ingredients. These are oxygen (from the air) and some heat to start the burning. When natural gas or coal burn, they mix with oxygen from the air to produce much more heat. At the same time, **water vapor**, **carbon dioxide** gas and sometimes soot are produced.

Smelly gas

Natural gas has no smell. This could be very dangerous because if you leave your gas stove on by mistake, your house would fill up with natural gas (instead of air) and you could suffocate. To avoid this, gas companies add a tiny amount of a substance called methyl mercaptan, which gives natural gas its smell.

Electricity

Electric appliances work in a different way. The electrical energy comes through the power lines to your house. The electricity flows through metal coils called elements in stoves, ovens, toasters and electric jugs. Special metals are chosen to make these coils. These metals are very good at changing electrical energy into heat energy.

Microwaves

Microwave ovens are powered by electricity, but they work in a different way. Inside is a tube called a magnetron. It gives off invisible waves (a bit like radio waves). When the waves hit the food, they make the water inside the food **vibrate** and bounce around. All the water bouncing around causes **friction** which then heats up the food.

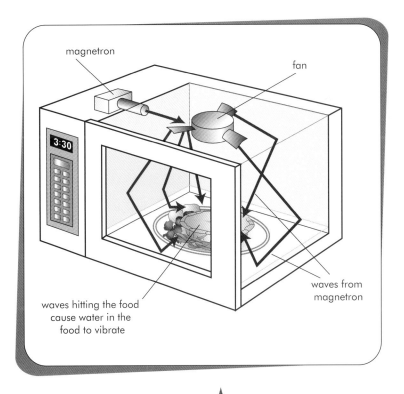

magnetron

fan

3:30

waves hitting the food cause water in the food to vibrate

waves from magnetron

Natural gas provides energy for cooking.

A microwave oven cooks food by causing friction.

Kitchen chemicals

Try this

Long words are easier to say if you break them down into smaller parts. Try to say these chemical words. (The first one has been broken into smaller bits for you.)

1 pyrethrins:
py—reth—rins
(This chemical is used to kill insects.)

2 calcium carbonate
(This is the chemical name for chalk.)

3 polyethylene terephthalate
(A tricky one! This is used to make plastic drink bottles.)

Science term

Proteins are a group of chemicals found in all living things.

Your kitchen is full of chemicals.

Did you know that everything around you is made from chemicals? Food is made of chemicals, the air is a mixture of chemicals and so is the water you drink.

Some chemicals have very long names. This is because there are so many chemicals that scientists made up a special system to name them all.

Some chemicals in your kitchen

Common name	Chemical name
Water	dihydrogen monoxide
Vinegar	ethanoic acid
Chili	capsaicin
Baking soda	sodium hydrogen carbonate
Salt	sodium chloride
Bleach	sodium hypochlorite
Natural gas	methane
Vitamin C	ascorbic acid
Cling wrap	polyethene

Most things in your kitchen are mixtures of many different chemicals. For example, milk contains more than 20 chemicals.

Chemicals in food

All the foods you eat are mixtures of chemicals. Fats, **proteins** and carbohydrates are all chemicals. So are vitamins and minerals.

Natural colors and flavors in foods are also chemicals. Chlorophyll is the name of the chemical that makes green vegetables green. Pentyl acetate is the name of a chemical that makes bananas smell like bananas.

Some chemicals are found naturally in the air, water and soil or in plants and animals. Sugar is an example of a natural chemical. It is **extracted** from the sugar cane plant. Chemicals that are made in factories or laboratories are called synthetic or artificial chemicals. A sweetener like saccharine is made in a factory.

Meet a food scientist

Have you ever asked yourself what it would be like to work in the food industry? What sorts of jobs are there? How is it possible to get a job? What do you have to study in high school and at college?

Meet Anne Sibbel

Anne Sibbel has the answers to these questions. She is a Coordinator of Consumer Science at a university.

Anne went to a high school that strongly promoted science, which is one of the reasons why she enjoyed it so much. In 12th grade she studied math, science and German. When Anne left school she studied at university and took a lot of different courses, including food technology and teaching.

Anne became interested in food science almost by accident. When she was 15, she was making Russian red cabbage salad. She accidentally tipped the water from the boiled eggs over the red cabbage and the water went a deep purple color. When she put the red cabbage in vinegar it changed back to red. Although this is a common experiment, Anne thinks that it started her fascination with the science of food.

Anne Sibbel is interested in the ingredients of foods.

Anne now works researching the ingredients in different foods. She is very interested in how foods can be developed for people with special needs. This includes people with allergies or who are unable to use a knife and fork. Anne also measures and describes the look, taste, feel and sound of foods. Some of her time is spent teaching food science. She likes to be able to help people to make choices about healthy and enjoyable foods.

Anne says that in food science there are so many ways your knowledge can be used. You can develop new food products, research food safety, work in companies who advertise and sell foods, and teach food science to others.

Are cakes really made of chemicals?

What is your favorite type of cake? Some cakes, such as fruit cakes, are heavy. Sponges are very light and fluffy. Have you ever baked a cake? They are nearly all made from the same basic ingredients. The ingredients are made of chemicals.

Mixing cake chemicals

To make a cake you need flour. Flour for cakes is made from ground-up wheat. To make a cake rise, you need to add a rising agent, like baking powder. Self-raising flour already has the rising agent added to it. You usually add sugar or honey to a cake to make it sweet. You can also use butter and eggs, which help to make the cake moist and rich tasting. Lastly, you need to add a liquid like milk or water to help mix all the ingredients together. When you add the milk or water, a **chemical reaction** begins. The baking powder starts to make bubbles of carbon dioxide gas.

Science term

A chemical reaction is a change in one or more substances to form new substances.

In the oven

When you put the cake mixture in the oven, the chemical reaction speeds up as the mixture is heated. More bubbles of carbon dioxide gas are made. The bubbles then get bigger because the gas inside them **expands** as it gets hotter. But the bubbles do not burst because the heat also makes the egg and the flour in the cake mixture set. This traps the air and carbon dioxide so the cake ends up full of tiny bubbles. These bubbles make the cake spongy and light.

You can see the holes made by the gas that formed when this sponge cake was cooked.

Baking powder

Baking powder is a mixture of two chemicals. One is called sodium bicarbonate and the other is tartaric acid. When you put them in water a chemical reaction happens. The mixture fizzes because the chemicals react to make carbon dioxide gas. The gas bubbles out of the mixture. You can write this chemical reaction as a sentence:

sodium bicarbonate + tartaric acid ➞ sodium tartrate + carbon dioxide + water

The words on the left side of the arrow in a chemical reaction are the ingredients, and the words on the right side are the things that form after the reaction happens. The arrow shows that a reaction has happened.

Bread

Bread is also full of tiny bubbles, but they are formed in a different way. To make bread you use wheat or rye flour and water. People usually use yeast instead of baking powder to make the bread rise.

Yeast is a type of fungus that is very small and very useful in the kitchen. Because yeast is a living thing, you have to treat it carefully. If you feed it sugar and keep it warm, it grows and multiplies. This is done by 'resting' the bread dough before you bake it. As the yeast grows, it releases carbon dioxide gas. The gas bubbles get trapped in the bread dough, which makes the bread rise. When you bake the bread dough in a hot oven, the yeast dies because it is too hot. The bread dough cooks, and the bubbles of carbon dioxide are trapped.

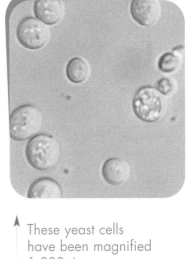

These yeast cells have been magnified 1,000 times.

Science fact

Other yeasty feasts

Yeast is the rising agent for crumpets, bagels and pizza dough. Yeast is also used to give sparkling wine its bubbles.

The holes in bread are made by bubbles of carbon dioxide.

How do your senses work?

What is your favorite food? Do you like its taste or its smell? Do you like it because it feels good in your mouth or because it brings back a good memory?

Food is important, because without it you would not have the energy to stay alive and grow. Food is also important because it brings pleasure. People enjoy eating food with friends, they enjoy special foods on birthdays or at other celebrations. People may even give special food for presents. To enjoy food, you need your senses.

Taste and smell

You taste and smell food every day. In the past, people had to taste and smell food to survive. They would recognize the smell of food that was poisonous or bad. Your senses of smell and taste work in a similar way. When you breathe in a smell or put a taste in your mouth, special **sensors** in your nose and on your tongue send messages to your brain. Your brain recognizes the smell or taste and you think 'fish and chips for dinner' or 'what a tasty apple'.

The nose knows

There are more than 10 million smell sensors in your nose. They are deep inside your nasal cavity (a big space behind your nostrils), just underneath your brain. When tiny smell particles go up your nose, they attach to the smell sensors. This sends a message to your brain and you recognize the smell immediately. Most people can smell about 4,000 different odors. A person with a well-trained nose (such as a perfume tester) can smell about 10,000 different odors.

Would you eat this?

Your nose is a very sensitive instrument.

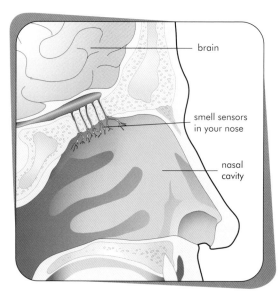

brain

smell sensors in your nose

nasal cavity

Good taste

Look at your tongue in a mirror. It is covered with thousands of tiny bumps. These are *not* your taste buds! These are called papillae. Most of your taste buds are in the grooves between your papillae. Each taste bud is a bunch of about 50 taste sensors.

There are four main types of taste sensors. They taste sweet (like sugar), salty (like salt), sour (like vinegar) and bitter (like strong black coffee). Everything you taste is a mixture of just four tastes. Some scientists believe there is another type of taste sensor called 'umami', which senses 'meaty' tastes.

Your taste buds are too small to be seen. The bumps on your tongue are called papillae.

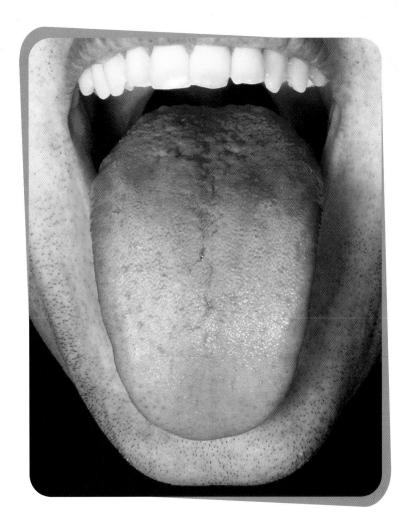

Changing taste

You are born with about 10,000 taste buds. As you grow older, some of your taste buds die. That is why some foods may taste stronger to children than they do to adults. Lots of children hate broccoli or brussels sprouts but love them when they grow up. Children usually like sweet foods but, as they grow older, may develop a taste for other foods. What you like often depends on what you became used to as a child.

Why are chilies hot?

Chilies and foods that contain chilies burn your mouth. They can also burn your eyes and skin if you are not careful when you are cutting them up. The thing that burns is a chemical called capsaicin. Capsaicin activates the pain sensors on your skin and in your mouth. So you feel pain when you eat chilies.

Science fact

Losing your sense of smell

Loss of hearing is called deafness. What if you lose your sense of smell? It is called anosmia. People with anosmia say that they do not enjoy their food very much. They also miss out on memories that come back when you smell something. Anosmia can also be quite dangerous because you cannot smell food that is spoiled or burning on the stove.

The amount of 'heat' in a chili depends on the type of chili and the part of the chili that is eaten.

Do you know why people eat food? There are several reasons. People eat food to get the fuel that gives them the energy to live. They also eat to get the raw materials to grow, repair their bodies and reproduce.

Fuel

Just as you put gasoline in your car to make it go, you have to put food in your body to keep it going. Food gives you the energy you need to move, to think and to stay alive. Remember that energy cannot be created or destroyed. It can only be changed from one form into another.

Food contains stored chemical energy. When you digest your food, a chemical reaction happens and the stored chemical energy is changed into heat (to keep your body at the right temperature) or movement (to pump blood around your body or to move your leg muscles, for example).

Different foods contain different amounts of energy. Energy is usually measured in calories. The number of calories in processed foods is sometimes shown on their packages.

Science fact

Chocolate fuel

Celery is a low-energy food, but chocolate is a high-energy food. You could walk all day on the energy in one chocolate bar.

Can you see how much energy is shown on this food label?

Nutrition Facts

Serving Size 2/3 cup (166g)
Servings Per Container About 2.5

Amount Per Serving

Calories 160   Calories from Fat 5

% Daily Value*

Total Fat 0.5g	0%
Saturated Fat 0g	0%
Cholesterol 0mg	0%
Sodium 35mg	1%

PACKED FOR F
ARLINGTON H

TO MAINTAIN P
OPENING, REFR
GLASS OR F

WHEN CORR
PLEASE INCL
THE CODE

Science fact

Banana energy

Bananas contain sugars and starch, which give you energy. Sugars and starch belong to a group of chemicals called carbohydrates. A banana gives you about 110 calories of energy. This is enough energy to walk quickly for about 10 minutes.

Raw materials

When you put food into your body, energy is not the only thing you get out of it. Food contains the raw materials that you need to grow and repair your body. You need lots of different raw materials to stay healthy.

For example, you need:

⊙ proteins to grow your hair, heal wounds and replace skin cells that flake off

⊙ calcium and vitamin D to keep your bones strong and healthy

⊙ fats and oils keep your skin from drying out

⊙ fiber to keep your digestive system going

⊙ iron for healthy blood.

To make sure that you get all the raw materials to keep your body in good shape, you should always eat a variety of foods. Dieticians are scientists who help prevent and treat illnesses caused by poor nutrition.

These foods provide energy and raw materials to keep you healthy.

Caffeine

There are some things in food that do not give you energy for your muscles and that are not the raw materials needed to grow and repair your body. Tea, coffee, chocolate and some soft drinks contain a chemical called caffeine. People often drink tea or coffee to keep them awake and alert. The caffeine makes your heart beat faster. Too much caffeine can give you a headache, keep you awake at night and make you grumpy.

Microorganisms

Have you ever left the milk out of the refrigerator by mistake? It goes lumpy and smells awful. If you leave an orange for long enough it will grow a green powdery mold all over it. You could leave uncooked rice out for months and months and nothing would happen to it. Some foods seem to go bad a lot more quickly than others. In the end, all uneaten foods will go bad. This is important because when foods go bad, they **decompose** and **nutrients** are returned to the soil. Some people keep compost bins to turn food scraps into fertilizer for gardens.

What makes food go bad?

All around you in the air and on everything you touch are tiny living things. They are so small that they can be seen only through a powerful microscope. They are called microorganisms. Like all living things, microorganisms need food to grow and reproduce. They also need water, and they grow best when it is not too hot or not too cold. The two main types of microorganisms that make food go bad are bacteria and molds.

Microbiologists study microorganisms such as bacteria and molds. These scientists help us to understand new ways to prevent food from going bad.

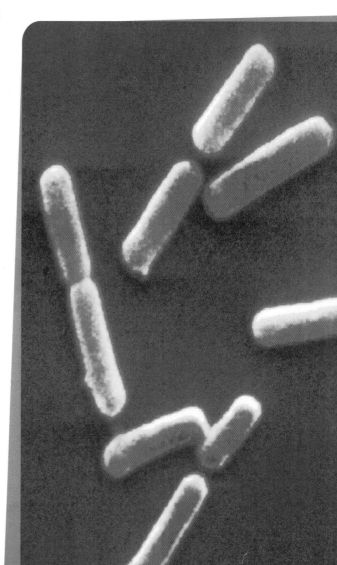

Bacteria are microorganisms. These bacteria have been magnified 18,000 times. →

16

Bacteria

Bacteria are everywhere—in the air, on the surfaces in your house and on your skin. Bacteria get onto your food when you or something else touches it, or if you leave food uncovered. Mostly this does not cause a problem because the bacteria are harmless and there are not too many of them. If the bacteria start to grow and multiply on your food, then they can become a problem. They use up nutrients in the food to grow and give off bad-smelling and sometimes poisonous wastes.

Baby bacteria

Most humans wait until they are at least 18 years old before they have children. Bacteria wait only 20 minutes. If the conditions are right, every 20 minutes a single bacterium splits in two. Twenty minutes later those two split in two, so now you have four bacteria. After 1 hour you have eight bacteria. After 2 hours there are 64 bacteria. So if you left a warm piece of chicken out of the refrigerator overnight (say for 8 hours), one bacterium would have multiplied into nearly 17 million bacteria!

Molds

Have you ever seen an orange covered in powdery green stuff, or a piece of bread that has gone green and hairy? They are each being attacked by mold, which is different from bacteria. Molds are types of fungus and belong to the same group of living things as mushrooms. Blue cheese is blue because mold is deliberately put into it while it is being made.

Science fact

Stinky spuds

One of the worst smells you can smell is a rotting potato. The particular bacteria that attacks potatoes breaks down the potato and makes some of the same chemicals found in horse manure. Which explains why it smells so bad!

Bacteria double every 20 minutes.

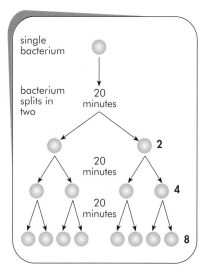

single bacterium

bacterium splits in two — 20 minutes

20 minutes — 2

20 minutes — 4

8

Mold can cause food to go bad.

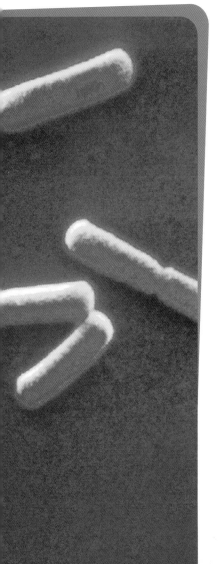

Keeping food cool

One way to stop bacteria growing in your food is to keep it cool. Bacteria live and reproduce best in moderate temperatures. They do not like very hot or very cold temperatures. Putting food in your refrigerator does not kill bacteria, but it slows down their growth. A freezer is even better.

Early refrigerators used big blocks of ice to keep food cool.

Refrigerators

Refrigerators keep your food and drinks cold. You need to keep some foods, like meat and milk, cold so that they do not go bad. You may refrigerate other things, like drinks, because they are more refreshing if they are cold, especially on a hot day. Refrigerators work by using evaporation and condensation.

Evaporation

Try wetting the back of your hand and blowing across it. What did you feel? The moving air across the top of your hand helped the moisture evaporate quickly. When a liquid such as water evaporates, this means it has turned into a gas. One way of turning a liquid into a gas is to heat it. The liquid on the back of your hand took heat from your body to help it to evaporate. That is why your hand felt cooler.

Condensation

Condensation is the opposite of evaporation. When a gas turns back into a liquid it is called condensation. When this happens heat is given off. You can see condensation at work when you breathe onto a mirror. The warm water vapor in your breath condenses into drops of water when it touches the cold mirror.

How does my refrigerator work?

Inside your refrigerator are two connected pipes. You can sometimes see one of the pipes coiled at the back. Inside the pipes is a liquid called a refrigerant. There is an electric pump that forces the refrigerant around the pipes. The refrigerant absorbs heat from the food compartment, which makes it evaporate (turn into a gas). The refrigerant gas then moves to the back of the refrigerator, where the pump forces it under high pressure to condense (turn back into a liquid). When this happens heat is given out at the back. The refrigerant liquid is then used again to remove more heat from the food.

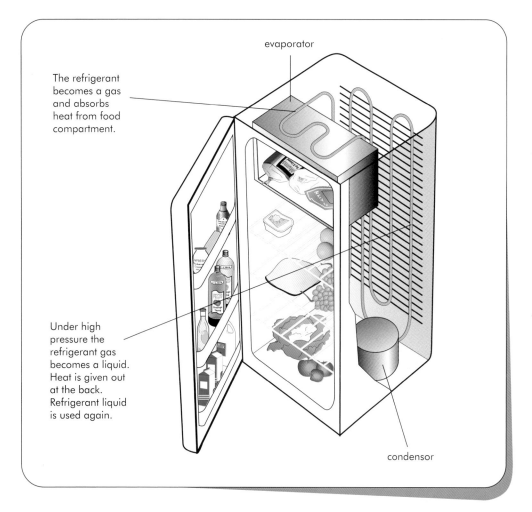

evaporator

The refrigerant becomes a gas and absorbs heat from food compartment.

Under high pressure the refrigerant gas becomes a liquid. Heat is given out at the back. Refrigerant liquid is used again.

condensor

Refrigerators work by removing heat from the food compartment.

Freezing food and drink

Water is one of the strangest chemicals in the world. It behaves in a very unusual way when it **freezes** and turns into ice. When most other liquids freeze, they shrink, but when water freezes it gets bigger—it expands. Have you ever left a full bottle of drink in the freezer by mistake? When it freezes, the expanding drink pops the lid off and sometimes even breaks the bottle. This expansion is the reason why some foods cannot be frozen successfully.

What did people do without refrigerators?

When people buy food, they usually put it in the refrigerator or freezer to keep it fresh. Refrigerators have been around for just over 100 years. So what did people do before this? Imagine that you went fishing and caught ten times more fish than you could eat, but you could not put the leftovers in the refrigerator. What if all the apricots on your apricot tree were ripe at once? How could you store them without them going bad?

For many centuries people have worked out ways to keep food from going bad. They found that you could dry the food, make it into jam or pickles, or add spices or salt and it would last much longer. This is called preserving.

It is possible to preserve all sorts of fruit and vegetables.

Think about how long these things would last if they were kept out of the refrigerator:

- an apricot compared to a jar of apricot jam
- a cucumber compared to a jar of pickled cucumbers
- a fresh corn cob compared to a packet of popping corn.

Jam lasts longer than fresh fruit because it has lots of sugar added. Pickles last a long time because they are in vinegar. Popping corn has been dried and contains less water than fresh corn.

How preserving works

Hardly anybody lives in Antarctica or in very hot deserts. This is because it is too cold or too hot, and there is not enough food or drinking water around. Just like people, bacteria and molds grow best when the temperature and the food are just right. This information can be used to help preserve food. You can kill bacteria and molds by cooking or chilling food. Drying foods by adding salt, sugar or vinegar takes out the water needed by bacteria or molds to grow, and kills them.

Spices

Curry contains lots of spices. Spices contain chemicals called anti-oxidants, which kill bacteria. So if you curry meat, it will not go bad so quickly. If the meat does go a bit bad, the strong flavor of the curry hides the bad taste. Hundreds of years ago, it was just as important to have spices in your kitchen as it is for people now to have a refrigerator.

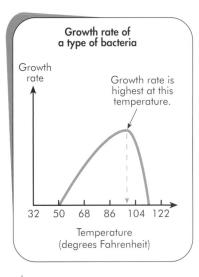

Growth rate of a type of bacteria

Growth rate

Growth rate is highest at this temperature.

32 50 68 86 104 122

Temperature (degrees Fahrenheit)

This bacteria grows best at body temperature.

Famous scientist

Louis Pasteur

When cows are milked, bacteria get into the milk. Some of these bacteria can cause diseases. Others can eventually make the milk go bad. If you boil milk, the bacteria are killed, but boiling makes the milk taste different.

In the 1860s a French man named Louis Pasteur (1822–1895) discovered how to kill the bacteria in milk without changing the taste of the milk. The milk is warmed up to 144 degrees Fahrenheit (62 degrees Celsius) for 30 minutes or 162 degrees Fahrenheit (72 degrees Celsius) for 15 minutes, and is then cooled quickly. The bacteria die, so the milk becomes safe to drink and it lasts longer before it goes bad. This process is called pasteurization.

Many spices are used in curries.

Try this

1 Ask an adult to boil some milk and then cool it again in the refrigerator.

2 Then ask them to pour you two glasses of milk—one that has been boiled and one that has not.

3 Taste each one. Can you tell the difference?

Food processing

If you eat an apricot straight off a tree, then you are eating food that is fresh. Canned apricots have been in a factory. They have had ingredients like water and sugar added to them, and they have been cooked. They are no longer fresh—they have been processed.

Why is food processed?

Sometimes food is processed so that it lasts longer. For example, fruit ripens at a particular time of the year. If it is cooked in sugar and water and put in cans, the canned fruit can be available at any time of the year.

Other food is prepared in a factory to save you time and energy. Hundreds of years ago, people used to make their own flour from wheat. This took so much time and energy that you could not do much else for the day.

Some things are cooked in the factory so you do not have to cook them at home. Other things like breakfast cereals, soft drinks, chocolate bars and some sandwich spreads you would probably never make at home.

Processed food is often designed for convenience.

22

Food additives

Processed foods often contain ingredients that you would not normally use if you were cooking at home. They are chemicals called food additives and are put into the food for many different reasons. Some are colorings or flavorings. Some are artificial sweeteners. Preservatives and antioxidants make the food last longer before it goes bad. Thickeners make liquids like sauces or ice cream thicker. Humectants stop foods from drying out and anticaking agents help powdery foods like salt to flow freely and keep the particles from sticking together.

So that you know what you are eating, these additives have to be listed on the food's packaging by law. Sometimes numbers are used instead of names because their names are too long to fit on the packet!

Some foods have colorings added to enhance their apperance.

Weird science

Did you know that one of the things that is added to cheese-flavored corn chips is sand? Sand has the chemical name silicon dioxide. Why do you think they put sand in corn chips? It is not to make them more crunchy. The cheese flavor is sprayed onto the chips. The sand stops the cheese flavor from clogging up the spraying machine.

INGREDIENTS: ENRICHED PARBOILED LONG GRAIN RICE (NIACIN, REDUCED IRON, THIAMINE MONONITRATE, RIBOFLAVIN, FOLIC ACID), SALT, NATURAL FLAVOR, DEHYDRATED VEGETABLES (ONION, BELL PEPPER, GARLIC), AUTOLYZED YEAST, YEAST EXTRACT, CHICKEN FAT, MONOSODIUM GLUTAMATE, DISODIUM INOSINATE AND DISODIUM GUANYLATE, TUMERIC, CAYENNE, TBHQ, (A PRESERVATIVE).

Numbers and names are used for the ingredients in this packet.

How does detergent do its work?

Have you ever tried to wash dishes without using any dishwashing detergent? The dishes stay greasy. Have you noticed that some salad dressing separates and the oil floats on the top?

Both of these things happen because oil and water do not mix. Oil is less dense than water so it floats on the top.

Soaps and detergents

The reason that soaps and detergents are used for washing is because they help the oil to mix with the water. Their active ingredient is a special tiny soap particle, or soap molecule, which loves both water and oil.

One end of the soap particle likes water and the other end likes oil or grease. When these particles are near a greasy plate, their oil-loving tails stick into the grease and their water-loving heads stick out and attract water. So the oil can mix with the water and be washed off more easily.

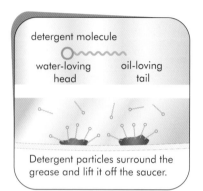

detergent molecule

water-loving
head

oil-loving
tail

Detergent particles surround the grease and lift it off the saucer.

When you put a greasy saucer into soapy water the tails of the soap particles, which hate water, stick into the grease. This lifts the grease off the saucer.

Detergent helps to remove the oil from dirty dishes.

Why do soap and detergent make bubbles?

If you fill a cup up with water so that it is almost overflowing, you can slide a paperclip onto the surface and it will float on top of the water. The paperclip floats because water has a high surface tension. A good way to understand surface tension is to imagine that there is a thin 'skin' on the water.

Detergents and soaps change the skin on the water. They lower the surface tension and the skin becomes weaker. It is very difficult to float a pin on a cup of soapy water because it falls through the weaker skin.

Plain water does not make bubbles because the surface tension is too strong. If you blow air into the water, the skin squeezes out the air and the bubble bursts straight away. With soapy water the air is not squeezed out because the skin is much weaker.

Both of these liquids are made from oil and vinegar. Which of these products also contains egg?

Salad dressing and mayonnaise

Many types of salad dressing are made from oil and vinegar with spices and flavors added. The oil and vinegar separate out. You have to shake up the mixture before you pour it on your salad. Mayonnaise is made from oil and vinegar, but it does not separate. The secret is that mayonnaise also contains eggs. Eggs contain chemicals called  that work the same way as the detergent molecules.

Science term

An emulsion is a mixture of oil and water that does not separate out. This is because it contains an emulsifier.

Homogenized milk

Milk contains fat and oils, which are called cream. Many years ago milk was sold in glass bottles and you could see the cream at the top of the milk (like the oil rises to the top in salad dressing). This does not happen anymore because milk is homogenized. Homogenizing is a high-pressure mixing of the milk that forces the cream into tiny globules that do not separate out. This is because milk also contains chemicals that work like detergent molecules.

Kitchen tools

Have you ever tried to open a can without a can opener, or cut bread without a knife? There are all sorts of tools in your kitchen to help you to prepare and eat your food. Many kitchen tools use levers or gears to help you do a particular job.

Levers

Some can openers are levers. All levers have a pole or bar that is stiff. It can rotate around a point that is called the fulcrum. The fulcrum on the can opener is the part that hooks under the rim of the can. The load is the thing that you are trying to move, in this case it is the metal top of the can. The effort is what you do to make that load move. You pull up on the other end of the opener. In a can opener, the load and the fulcrum are very close together. The farther away the effort is from the fulcrum, the easier it is to open the can.

Scissors, tongs, nutcrackers and garlic presses are double levers and the hinge is the fulcrum.

Chopsticks

Chopsticks have been used for eating in China for the past 3,500 years. They are still the main eating tools in China, Korea, Vietnam and Japan. Chopsticks are levers. Chopsticks are usually made from wood or bamboo, and these days they are also made from plastic. More than 45 billion pairs of disposable chopsticks are thrown away in China every year. Japanese chopsticks are usually thinner and pointier than Chinese chopsticks.

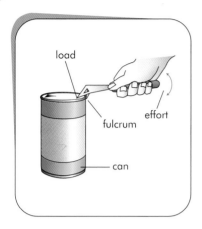

Some can openers are levers.

Science fact

Updating chopsticks

Bill Allardyce invented special chopsticks to help people who had trouble learning to use them. They are made of plastic and have a joint at the top that acts like a spring. The tips are rough so that they grip the food.

Chopsticks are levers.

Gears

A hand beater uses gears to increase the speed of the beaters and also to change the direction of movement.

Gears are toothed wheels that lock together. In a hand beater, there is one big gear wheel that you turn with the handle. It locks together with two small gear wheels, one for each beater. There are more teeth on the big gear wheel than the small gear wheels. So one turn of the big gear wheel makes the small gear wheels attached to the beaters turn five or six times faster. To whip cream or eggwhites, the beaters have to spin as fast as possible.

Can you see the gears on this hand beater?

Wedges

A knife is a type of wedge. If you look at a knife closely, it is thin and pointed on the cutting side of the blade and thicker on the other side. A wedge helps you to push things apart. The narrower the wedge (the sharper its point) the more easily it pushes something apart. So a really sharp knife has a really narrow wedge and it cuts easily. Chisels and axes are also wedges.

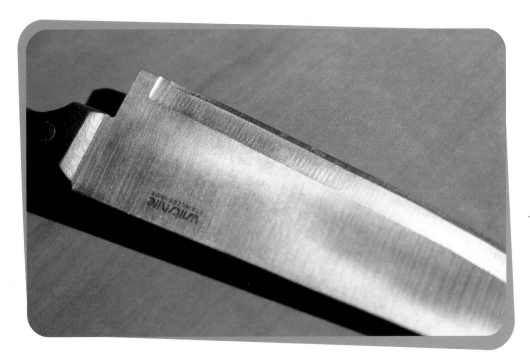

You can easily see the wedge on the cutting edge of this knife.

Kitchen safety

What are the hazards in your kitchen? A hazard is something that might cause an accident if it is not handled properly. A sharp knife can be a hazard because it can cut you. A stove can be a hazard because it can burn you or cause a fire. Some of the chemical cleaners in your kitchen are hazards because they are poisonous. If you know how to use all of the things in your kitchen safely you will reduce your risk of having an accident.

Fire in the kitchen

For a fire to start and stay burning it needs three things. They are heat, fuel and oxygen. To put out a fire, you need to take away one or more of these things.

Burning oil

One of the most common types of fires in kitchens is an oil fire. These fires usually happen when oil that is being used for frying food ignites.

The best way to put out burning oil is to smother the flames with a tight-fitting lid or a fire blanket. A fire blanket is made from a special fiberglass fabric that does not burn. By covering the fire, you are removing the oxygen, so the fire goes out. If you had one, you could also use a special fire extinguisher which is designed for oil fires. It contains foam, not water. The foam removes the oxygen by covering the fire, just like a fire blanket.

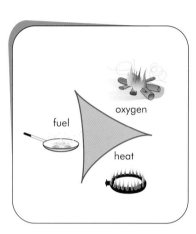

A fire needs heat, fuel and oxygen.

Science fact

Warning!

You should never put water on an oil fire. If you do, the water will boil immediately. This will cause the oil to splatter everywhere and the fire may spread.

Electrical fires

If any electrical appliance like your toaster or oven ignites, it is called an electrical fire. Water is a good electrical conductor. This means that the electricity can travel along the water to you. If it passes through your body, you can be badly injured or killed. If there is an electrical fire, you should turn off the power at the main circuit board if it is safe to do so. Only if the power has been turned off should you cover the fire with a fire blanket. There are also special fire extinguishers for electrical fires.

Smoke detectors

Smoke is made up of gases and tiny particles. Smoke detectors are like electronic noses. They can sense small amounts of invisible smoke particles. Inside most household smoke detectors is a space filled with air. There is a tiny amount of electricity flowing through it. When the smoke gets into the space, it changes the electricity flow. This automatically switches on a very loud beep to warn you about a fire. Your sense of smell partly shuts down at night when you are asleep. So you cannot smell smoke as easily as you can when you are awake. That is why it is important to have smoke detectors near bedrooms.

Science fact

Warning!

You should never put water on an electrical fire. If you do, you could get a bad electric shock.

Safe kitchens contain fire-warning equipment and fire-extinguishing equipment.

Kitchen science timeline

This timeline shows some important kitchen science events. See if you can imagine some of the things that might happen in kitchen science in the future.

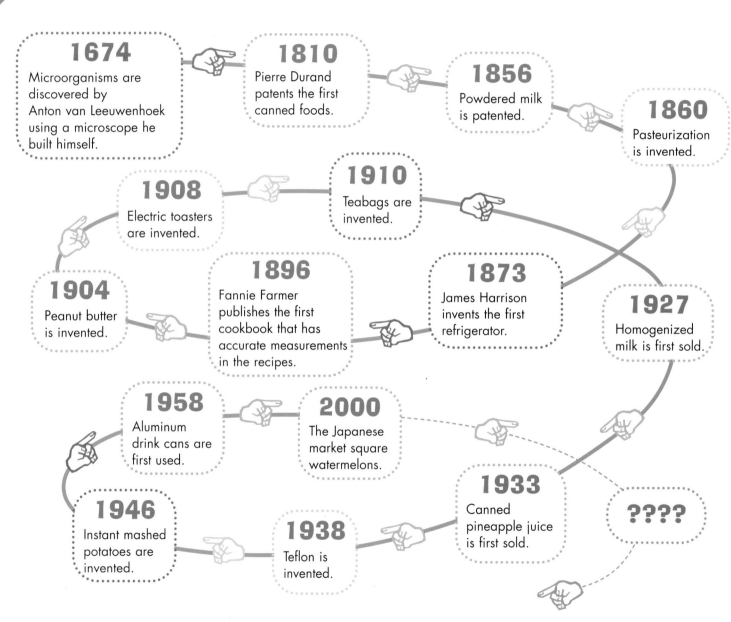

1674
Microorganisms are discovered by Anton van Leeuwenhoek using a microscope he built himself.

1810
Pierre Durand patents the first canned foods.

1856
Powdered milk is patented.

1860
Pasteurization is invented.

1908
Electric toasters are invented.

1910
Teabags are invented.

1904
Peanut butter is invented.

1896
Fannie Farmer publishes the first cookbook that has accurate measurements in the recipes.

1873
James Harrison invents the first refrigerator.

1927
Homogenized milk is first sold.

1958
Aluminum drink cans are first used.

2000
The Japanese market square watermelons.

1933
Canned pineapple juice is first sold.

????

1946
Instant mashed potatoes are invented.

1938
Teflon is invented.

What are scientists working on now?

⊙ Testing is underway on a robot that can make pancakes for restaurants.

⊙ Scientists are trying to make chewing gum that is chewy but not sticky.

⊙ A substance has been identified in cinnamon that may help to cure a type of diabetes.

Glossary

bacteria	microscopic living organisms (When there is only one it is called a bacterium.)
carbon dioxide	a gas that is produced by animals and taken in by plants
chemical reactions	changes in one or more substances to form new substances
decompose	to decay or rot
energy	the ability of an object to do work. Energy cannot be created or destroyed, but it can be changed from one form to another
expands	increases in size
extracted	removed or taken out
friction	a force created when one surface moves over another surface. Smooth surfaces have lower friction than rough surfaces
fungi	living organisms, like a mushroom or mold, that are neither plants nor animals
nutrients	substances that are necessary for living things to survive
nutrition	the study of food and how living things use it
organisms	living things, including plants, animals, bacteria and fungi
proteins	the name for a group of chemicals found in all living things
sensors	instruments that detect changes in the surrounding environment
vibrate	shake from side to side
water vapor	the gaseous state of water

Index